ROAD TO $10K ROAD MAP

*How to Make $10,000 a Week by Starting
Your Own Box Truck Delivery Business*

Monique Gilliam

Acknowledgments

This book is dedicated to all of those that had my back during my shortcomings while building my business.

To my mom: You instilled the hustle in me and taught me to never give up because there is no such thing as "can't."You can do anything you put your mind and effort to.

To Dude: You had my back no matter what ideas I came up with. You always had the right words to say when I was feeling overwhelmed, and I am very grateful to have you in my corner.

Special shout out to my cousin Corey, my number 1 fan and biggest supporter of them all.

I love yall, and without your support, I wouldn't have made it this far.

Contents

CHAPTER 1

Mental Preparation

You may have already watched hundreds of videos on trucking or googled until you can't google anymore, and, at this point, you are probably wondering if this trucking business is even for you. Well, let me answer that question for you. Starting your own business, no matter what it might be, takes a certain mindset and determination. You have to be mentally prepared for all the ups and downs that come with starting and operating a business.

Starting your own trucking business is for those that want to gain experience daily. You have to be willing to take the necessary steps to be your own boss and have that financial freedom you dream of. This venture is not for those that are not willing to risk it all. It's a lot of hard work and sleepless nights, but the end all be all is totally worth it.

Some people are going to think you're crazy for giving up your 9 to 5 to chase your dreams, but my motto is, if you can dedicate 8 hours a day to your current job, then you can dedicate that same time to building your own empire.

In order to be successful, you have to think about success. Don't let the smallest bump in the road deter you from moving forward. It happens, and if anyone has told you that they never experienced any obstacles in their journey to building their business, then they are lying. There will be a lot of sleepless nights and wondering where you will get the money to even start or keep the business going. The first few months are the hardest when starting a business.

Whether you fail or succeed, depends on your determination and mindset, is that a chance you are willing to take? If not, then you may want to reconsider being an entrepreneur because I am here to tell you, this is not an easy venture.

Mindset 1: Project the idea of running a successful business

Preparing mentally for what's coming is essential for starting and running a successful trucking business. You may not have confidence in the beginning, and you might doubt yourself, but remember—only the strong ones go forward. Keep reminding yourself that this is what you've always wanted, and the time is finally here to prove to yourself, your family, and people around you that you can do this.

Achieving your goal shouldn't be in question. In fact, you should think of it as something that will happen soon, no matter the obstacles, the sleepless nights, or the energy you need to devote to building this business. Projecting this idea onto others will make them believe in you, and positive energy and enthusiasm are something everyone needs to move forward and never give up.

Put it this way: you've already tackled the most challenging step: deciding to follow your dreams, start your own business, and become your own boss. Now, it's time to build a name for yourself and create an empire. Of course, some days will be harder than others, but that doesn't mean you should slow down. It means you only need to double on effort!

Mindset 2: Get out of your comfort zone

I'm sure you've heard the saying, "Life begins at the end of your comfort zone," and that's true, especially if you are trying to make a big change in your life.

Remaining in your comfort zone and backing down from every risk, won't get you far as a business owner. You need to embrace those aspects of your trucking business that cause you discomfort and cause trouble because once you learn how to deal with problems, your mindset will expand, and you'll start to see real change in your life.

Feel uneasy asking for a business loan to start your journey? Partnering with a good finance company is something that will help you catapult your business. So, make those calls, and after some time, you'll come to recognize that awkward feeling and discomfort as an opportunity to do great things. That's when you'll start really breaking boundaries!

Remember this, like any other business, is not for those who aren't willing to go beyond their comfort zone. At the end of the day, remind yourself that starting this trucking business is something you are doing for yourself. Don't let fear come between you and your goal.

Mindset 3: Keep moving forward

Throughout your business journey, there will be disappointments, frustrations, and resentment. You may even consider stepping back or changing your goals. How you deal with stressful situations speaks a lot about you as an entrepreneur.

Tough times can test you, so don't think about giving up, even for a second. If you make a mistake, breathe, find a way to solve it, and learn from it. It is okay to lose your motivation and take a day off to gather your thoughts but always come back stronger and with eyes on the price.

Use all the resources at your disposal and send a message to the universe that you *are* moving this business forward. As long as you learn and grow, you'll see your goals turning into a reality.

Mindset 4: Ask yourself, "Do I really want this?"

If you don't love your job, sooner or later, you'll want to stop doing it, and you likely will! When you run your own business, you have to be 100% all-in. You can't run a business and make 10K or more if you are sitting and thinking about how great it will be doing something else.

No, the only way to succeed is to be absolutely sure you love what you do and that all of your efforts will pay off. If you can think of another job or another business project you'd rather do, you are in trouble.

On the other hand, if you are committed and mentally prepared, you are ready to build an empire and overcome all the difficulties that come with it. Just like a piano player prepares before a concert and runs the scales multiple times or an athlete stretches before a game, you have to put in the preparation necessary to run a trucking business.

CHAPTER 2

Business Preparation

"Where do I begin?" That's probably the most common question I get, and it's asked daily. For starters, please don't spend too much time on these steps because the most time-consuming part of starting your business comes in the form of footwork. I will provide the steps for you to get started. Set a time limit on how much time you will spend on each task, and when each checkpoint is completed, you will have completed the steps needed to form your business. Listed below is a 9-point checklist that will successfully help you form your trucking company.

9 Important Steps to Getting Your Box Truck Business Started

1. Form Your LLC

When forming your LLC, you want to think of a name that is unique and has meaning to you. You want to make sure it is relevant to trucking as well. You don't want to name your business J&J's Pink Panther, LLC, for example. What you do should be obvious from your company name. Examples of keywords you want to use to help others identify what you do include:

○ Carriers

○ Conveyors

○ Shippers

○ Transporters

○ Expediters

○ Trucking

So, in this example, "J&J's Trucking, LLC" would be a better choice. You also want to make sure no one else is using that exact same name.

2. Register Your Domain Name (Get your EIN#)

When applying for your EIN#, make sure all the information provided on your LLC matches the information on your EIN application. If you have special characters in your business name, it will not show on your EIN application. That's not a major problem.

3. Get the Right License for Your Trucking Business

To operate legally—which is pretty important—you'll need to get all the necessary licenses. The Department of Transportation (DOT) requires several forms to get your new trucking business up and running.

Like contracting or construction businesses need specific licenses and certificates to operate, you need one as well. Check with the local state business license office and get the documents ready to proceed to the next stage.

4. Get a Business Phone Number

A business phone number will allow you to distinguish your personal calls from your business calls, and it also shows a more professional look for your business.

5. Open a Business Bank Account

When applying for financing for your business, most lenders are going to want to see business bank statements. Even if you haven't started making money directly with the business, you can have whatever source of income you have at the time deposited into your business account.

6. Duns and Bradstreet

The Duns and Bradstreet number is used as your business social security number. This is where anything that is purchased with a net-30 account is reported to. Your Duns and Bradstreet number is very important if you are looking to build business credits for your business.

7. Create a Website

A professional website will allow you access to a lot of opportunities. Whether you are promoting your business or looking for financing, this website will come in handy. Most finance companies ask for the link to your website, which gives them insight into what your business has to offer and also gives your business that professional look.

Aside from building a more professional look, you can use your website to promote your business 24/7. Before you create any promotional campaigns, make sure your website design embodies your brand and company vision. Your website visitors should understand your business, who you are, and what's your story as soon as they click on your site.

Believe it or not, your website tells viewers a lot about your trucking business, including whether you provide the fastest service, the most reliable, the safest, and much more. When designing your website, make sure it projects your personality and business' uniqueness, and don't forget to:

● Use your logo's colors

● Write about how everything started (what inspired you to start your trucking business)

● Include an engaging copy with your target audience in mind

● Showcase your identity and what makes your company the best choice

8. Business email

Your business email is used just like the business phone number. You always want to distinguish the business from personal, and this email also gives your business a more professional feel and look.

9.   Get Insurance

Every truck you own should have insurance. When reviewing different types of insurance, you will come across general liability, cargo, and non-tracking liability insurance.

● **General liability** insurance protects your trucking business if a property or a person is damaged due to load delivery error, crash, and other accidents.

● **Cargo insurance** protects your trucking business from loss if the package is damaged or lost during shipping and delivery.

● **Non-trucking insurance** covers drivers between shifts or when using company vehicles for personal reasons.

You can also consider medical payment coverage, physical damage coverage, trailer coverage, and other types of insurance policies useful for trucking companies.

Knowing all possible logistical and legal considerations of running a trucking business will lay out a powerful foundation for your company's success in the future. Book a call to speak with me about starting your Box Truck business today and get on the **road to 10k.**

Chapter 3

Getting Started

Getting started and knowing where to start is the hardest part of starting your trucking career. My first authority—I screwed it up royally, but I learned from my mistakes. When I started again for the second time, it was a breeze.

I established my first authority in 2017. I thought I knew it all but boy was I wrong. I applied for my authority, got my BOC3, MC-150 and LLC. 21 days later, my authority was active, but there was only one problem. I DIDN'T have a truck, nor the required insurance needed for the authority. I was given 45 days to have insurance on some type of vehicle to keep my authority active. I never got the vehicle nor the insurance within those 45 days, so my authority went inactive.

Once I finally got everything active (6 months later), there were huge fines waiting on me. Now I'm even more devastated than I was 6 months earlier. Lucky for you, I'm going to provide you with step-by-step instructions to get started.

The very first thing you want to do is find a name for your business. After you have come up with the name, then get your LLC. Make sure your name matches on each document, or that will become a problem when working with the brokers and insurance companies.

Once you have your LLC, open a bank account. I found Wells Fargo and Bank of America the easiest to open a business account with. If you are looking to get business funding to purchase equipment or get a loan, you will need to show at least 3 months of business banking statements.

You will need a Duns and Bradstreet number to begin building your business credits, an EIN number (make sure the names match the previous documents I mentioned). Once you have completed those tasks, you can now begin to look for your truck.

Now that you have all your documents and are on the way to purchase your truck, there are a few forms you want to familiarize yourself with:

- MC150

- BOC3

- USDOT

These forms are very important because you will use them while applying for your authority. They are not needed until you actually have the truck and insurance and are close to getting on the road. I screwed up by having all these documents and no vehicle, and that's when I was hit with the fines to rectify that mistake.

CHAPTER 4

Finding the Right Truck

Finding the right truck is the most important factor throughout this entire guide. The type and size of the truck you have determine how much money you are able to make. When I first started, I started with a 15' truck, and let me be the first to tell you, that truck was equivalent to having a cargo van.

It was extremely hard to book loads that made sense monetarily. Of course, the fuel cost was more for that truck because it was bigger than a cargo van, but the loads paid cargo van rates. That's why choosing the right truck is very important. Just for the record, I prefer a Freightliner with a cummings engine, but that's just my preference for many reasons.

For starters, you want to know the specs of the vehicle, such as:

● **Height -** Your opening at the door should be at least 91 inches to allow the most general freight of regulated size to enter through the opening of the door.

• **Weight** - When purchasing a truck, you want to know the GVWR (gross vehicle weight rating). Your average box truck GVWR is 26,000 LBS. My suggestion: upon purchasing a truck, run it across the scale with a full tank of gas so that you know the exact weight you can carry.

• **Width** - The width of the truck should be at least 101 inches wide. This ensures there is enough width for standard pallets placed side by side.

• **Roll up or swing doors** - This is up to your preference. There are some loads that require swing doors over roll-up doors, but that won't hinder you if you decide to go with the swing doors.

• **Liftgate** - A liftgate is very important because some shippers and receivers don't have docks. The liftgate will assist with getting the freight in and out of the truck. Again, this is not a major factor when booking loads.

• **Air ride** - Air ride is also a preference. Some freight does require an air ride vehicle, and the pay is a little more, but again that's a preference at the owner's discretion.

- **E-tracks-** E-tracks is a must. They are used to secure the freight. You want to have at least 3 to 4 straps in the truck at all times.

The specs I have listed for you are very important. You don't have to have the exact measurements, but to ensure you are getting compensated with the best rates for your investment, you need a rough idea. The specs listed above will get you top dollar.

Outline a Vehicle Purchase Plan

If you want to get on the road to $10K, it is essential to have a long-term vehicle purchase strategy. Based on your previous experience in this industry, it is vital to choose the best vehicles for your fleet.

Don't forget to consider what your trucking business will haul, how many people will drive the trucks, and what types of roads your trucks will drive on. These things will help you think about crucial factors such as fuel costs, load capacity, and financial planning.

CHAPTER 5

Finance Companies

Coming into this business, we all don't have 20k-50k to drop on a vehicle, and that's where a finance company comes in. The finance company can help you secure either a business loan or finance the equipment you need to start your journey.

Remember earlier when I told you that you would need your business bank account open for three months? This is the reason why. In order to use a finance company for financing your truck or receive a business loan, they will want to see at least 3 months of those statements.

There are different types of business loans you can get from finance companies. One loan option is a daily withdrawal loan which is not based on your credit, but they will take a set amount from your account a day to pay this loan back. I don't recommend that type of loan unless you already have income coming in or you have income coming in within the next week because there is no grace period, and the daily deductions will begin as soon as the next business day. Finance companies also offer larger loans with longer terms to pay back, but of course, that is based on your credit.

So, to give you a sneak peek at how I purchased my first truck, I went through a company called National Biz Credit. They did a soft credit check and went through my business bank statements with a fine-tooth comb to ensure there were enough funds to cover the down payment and any extra taxes or expenses. The entire process took 2 weeks, but that was based upon me getting all the necessary documents back to them. After everything was in place and approved, I ended up putting down 7k. I also got them to finance my warranty in the deal because the warranty itself was an additional 4k. Below is the link if you would like to check out National Biz credit for business loans or financing your equipment.

https://partners.nationalbusinesscapital.com/partner/?ref=95970

CHAPTER 6

Dispatching and Working With Brokers

Let me just tell you this, if you have a brand-new authority, you will hear no a lot more than yes when you first start. Don't let that deter you from your goals because there is always light at the end of the tunnel. You will hear a lot of no's in the first 30 days of having your authority because a lot of brokers won't work with you until your authority is 60 days old.

Now there are some brokers that will work with you within the first 30 days, but the rates will be low. Take what you can and put your name behind your work. Would you rather turn down what you can get or make something until your authority has some age behind it?

Know your freight lanes. What I mean by that is know the hot areas that have constant freight. A load may be paying great to go to Cali, but how much fuel is it going to take to get there? What type of freight is coming out, and what is the DPM (dollar per mile) on the freight coming out? Just because you drove 3,000+ miles for a 4k payout doesn't always make it worth it when you could have stayed within an 800-mile radius and made the same amount with less fuel cost and less wear and tear on your vehicle.

When dealing with brokers, always negotiate. DO NOT TAKE THE FIRST OFFER because they always have more they can put on the deal. Incorporate your insurance cost, fuel cost, deadhead (the distance you have to drive to get the load), and day-to-day living cost in your negotiations.

Remember I said you will hear a lot of no's, so with that being said, don't just turn down a load because they didn't budge on the negotiation. You won't win them all, but you can't make any money if you shut down every load just because it didn't pay exactly what you wanted it to pay.

Once you have your own authority, you can basically dispatch yourself. There are several different load boards available to find loads. Paying a dispatcher to do what you can do on your own saves you $300-400 a week that you can reinvest into your business.

If you decide to dispatch yourself, please acquaint yourself with the difference between a partial load and a full load. Partial loads pay a lot less, but it gives you more room to add another partial load for additional money. Full loads pay more, but they tend to take up the entire truck, which is fine because it's worth the pay.

KNOW YOUR SPECS!!! KNOWING THE SPECS OF YOUR TRUCK WILL SAVE YOU FROM THE HEADACHE OF ARRIVING AT A SHIPPER, AND THE FREIGHT DOESN'T FIT!!!

CHAPTER 7

Factoring Companies

What is a factoring company, you may ask? A factoring company is a company you would use to purchase your invoices after you have completed a load. Unless you have money already saved up, you may want to use a factoring company.

The average time a broker has to pay you after completing a load can range anywhere from 30 to 60 days. The factoring company will purchase your invoices from the broker and pay you within 24 hours. The factoring company also has a feature where you can do a credit check on the broker prior to taking the load. Some brokers don't pass the credit check with the factoring company due to double brokering, and you want to steer clear of those brokers because you are at risk of not being paid.

When choosing a factoring company, be sure to do your research on that factoring company. Some factoring companies have high percentage rates, and that is sometimes due to what they offer. The factoring company I use has a 3% charge, but they offer non-recourse, a visa credit card with a revolving credit limit of up to 20k, and same-day payment depending upon the time you submit your documents, up to 50% of your funds upfront as well as fuel cards.

Choosing a factoring company that offers non-recourse is the most important to me. I once dealt with a factoring company that did not offer non-recourse, and when the broker didn't pay in a timely manner, I was charged for that invoice until the broker decided to pay. If the broker decided not to pay, then I took a load for free, but with non-recourse, you don't have to worry about if the broker pays or not. The factoring company will fight that fight for you. So, choosing the right factoring company is a big deal, and I will leave information for the company I use in the glossary.

Chapter 8

Building Business Credit

In the beginning, I mentioned Duns & Bradstreet and business credits. Building your business credit is just as important as building your personal credit. Building your business credit will help out tremendously with maintaining your business.

Building your business credit is not an overnight process. It takes time. There are certain tiers when building your business credit, and each tier has a certain dollar amount and number of vendors needed to work with to build the credit.

Once you have your business credit built to a certain tier, there are no limits to the doors you can open for your business. Business credit cards, fuel cards, as well as certain dealers can provide you with a line of credit to build your fleet.

There are some creditors that ask you for a personal guarantor, which means you basically allow them to run your personal credit before they make a decision.

Then there is a non-personal guarantor, which means the creditor only focuses on your Duns and Bradstreet profile to make a decision.

I personally use the non-personal guarantor option because I never mix business and personal due to legal reasons that can backfire on you personally. This decision is solely up to you because there are benefits to being a personal guarantor with your business.

Chapter 9

Create a Customer Base

Besides acquiring licenses, finding good trucks, and building your business credit, your new trucking business will need clients to get it running. For some company owners, this is the most challenging part, but for those who are mentally prepared and out of their comfort zones, this is nothing but a small obstacle to overcome.

A load board is one option, but once you start building your business, it helps to secure a larger customer base. At this point, marketing is an excellent tool to help you create buzz around your business and find more load leads. You can create a social media campaign to reach customers online, attend industry events to meet potential clients in person, or work on your website's blog so customers can learn more about your business.

When you secure that customer base, invest your energy into building long-lasting relationships. Nourishing your relationships with your clients can go a long way toward building an empire, and that is something every new business owner should aspire to. If customers are satisfied, they will spread the word about your business, and that's when the magic happens.

Chapter 10

Decrease Expenses

Now that you have a customer base and all documents ready, it is time to think about how you can decrease costs and achieve your goal of making $10K. The average cost to start a trucking business depends on what vehicle model you choose, any partners, and factoring companies, but overall, expect to need at least $10,000-$15,000.

A successful business owner should know when to cut costs and how to deal with upcoming expenses. One way to lessen operating costs and increase the cash flow is to use fleet management solutions such as Fleetio, Momentum IoT, USFleetTracking, or Onfleet. These systems decrease fuel costs, automate back-office processes, and improves truck efficiency.

Let's Wrap Things Up

For the brave men and women who dream about starting their own trucking business, this guide does include all steps to begin, build, and run one. If you do it right and believe in yourself, a trucking company may be the most life-changing and rewarding decision you'll ever make.

Are you ready to turn your dream into reality?

To learn more about getting started on your business credits, click on the link below and complete the short form to get more info. I greatly appreciate you all for taking the time to view the information. Now let's get you booked for your consultation, and you can be on your road to 10K!

About the Author

I started my trucking journey five years ago, and it definitely wasn't an easy journey. I've driven everything from tractor-trailers and dually trucks to box trucks, but the part I love most about trucking is helping others get their business started.

I decided to start a system to help others get all the info they need in one stop because if you are new to trucking, it can be quite overwhelming trying to figure out where to start. I will walk you step by step on starting your trucking career and hold your hand the entire ride—so let the journey begin!

DISCLAIMER: This is how I started my trucking company. These were my steps and my journey. There may be other simpler ways to get started, but this was how I made it happen.

Made in United States
North Haven, CT
05 January 2023

30623040R00026